T0207670

GODLY WISDOM FOR ALL

Living Life with Heaven in Mind

NATACHA MARTINO JOSSELIN

WESTBOW
PRESS®
A DIVISION OF THOMAS NELSON
& ZONDERVAN

Copyright © 2021 Natacha Martino Josselin.

All rights reserved. No part of this book may be used or reproduced by any means, graphic, electronic, or mechanical, including photocopying, recording, taping or by any information storage retrieval system without the written permission of the author except in the case of brief quotations embodied in critical articles and reviews.

This book is a work of non-fiction. Unless otherwise noted, the author and the publisher make no explicit guarantees as to the accuracy of the information contained in this book and in some cases, names of people and places have been altered to protect their privacy.

WestBow Press books may be ordered through booksellers or by contacting:

WestBow Press
A Division of Thomas Nelson & Zondervan
1663 Liberty Drive
Bloomington, IN 47403
www.westbowpress.com
844-714-3454

Because of the dynamic nature of the Internet, any web addresses or links contained in this book may have changed since publication and may no longer be valid. The views expressed in this work are solely those of the author and do not necessarily reflect the views of the publisher, and the publisher hereby disclaims any responsibility for them.

Any people depicted in stock imagery provided by Getty Images are models, and such images are being used for illustrative purposes only. Certain stock imagery © Getty Images.

Unless otherwise noted, all scripture taken from the New King James Version®. Copyright © 1982 by Thomas Nelson. Used by permission. All rights reserved.

ISBN: 978-1-6642-1403-3 (sc)
ISBN: 978-1-6642-1404-0 (hc)
ISBN: 978-1-6642-1402-6 (e)

Library of Congress Control Number: 2020923473

Print information available on the last page.

WestBow Press rev. date: 12/10/2020

CONTENTS

INTRODUCTION

I grew up in a secluded little town in Haiti, away from all the noise, and the neighbors were considered family. Most of them were Catholics, and the rest were Baptists. I was fortunate to grow up in a Christian environment.

Certain things were mandatory during my upbringing, such as attending church religiously. Growing up, I attended Christian schools and a strong Bible-believing Baptist Church, Eglise Baptiste Evangelique de Belle-Vue Thor, where they drilled and sealed the Word of God into my soul. I thank God for that.

I spent my childhood attending church services, participating in church events and activities, performing, singing, and acting out Bible stories on stage during Christmas and Easter. When I was in my early teenage years, things started to change. I began to understand and become aware that there had to be more than just attending church, singing, and performing Bible stories. I started longing for more. I believe that was God's way of opening my spiritual eyes to lead me to the real deal of conversion and to my personal walk with him. I didn't want to attend church as a routine or just to meet and hang out with friends anymore.

On the day I became a convert, a huge revival was happening just a few blocks away from my street. It was a beautiful revival. They were loud, and I could hear them praying and worshiping from many blocks away, which was unlike the Baptist church I grew up in or the type of worship I was accustomed to.

The revival took place in a large field. The people could stand up and worship or bring chairs. It was usually packed with people. That revival lasted at least two weeks. It came back for a few years before it stopped. I thank God they used to have it because one night I went to that revival and gave my life to Jesus as my Lord and Savior. From that point on, things were different. I continued going to my church, but I was still longing and searching for more.

I had begun to locate other Christian groups that used to gather outside in the open instead of inside the four walls of the church. Their worship was different; it was not scheduled or orchestrated like the church services I was used to. They could worship until they had no more strength left to look pretty. The prayers and the worship were intense, and they would not let go until they had felt moved by the Holy Spirit or had received a touch from God.

The outdoor church service would start early in the afternoon and go past midnight if it had to. I knew I had found a group of people who were as hungry for more of God—just like I was. These people were so on fire for God that a voodoo priest used to complain to Brother Robinson, the worship leader, and threaten him because he said our worship interfered with his voodoo ceremony. He asked Brother Robinson to stop the worship, but Brother Robinson was not afraid or bothered. The worship service continued as planned, which was a blessing for me and for many other people.

I hope and pray that my conversion story will help many people who have been going to church all their lives. They know all the hymns and the scriptures, but they have never actually had an encounter with Jesus to surrender to him. May you be set free from the religious spirit and come to accept Jesus as your Lord and Savior. Without being born again and having a relationship with Jesus, all other church activities are done in vain. May you come to know Christ so deeply that you have a personal relationship with him. May you stay hungry for more. No matter how close you think you are in your relationship with God, there's always much more to learn about and to experience with God.

> Abide in Me, and I in you. As the branch cannot bear fruit of itself, unless it abides in the vine, neither can you, unless you abide in Me. I am the vine, you are the branches. He who abides in Me, and I in him, bears much fruit; for without Me you can do nothing. (John 15:4–5)

ACKNOWLEDGMENTS

First and foremost, above all else, I would like to acknowledge my absolute best and closest friend—my Lord and Savior Jesus Christ—for his everlasting, unconditional love, grace, favor, and mercies toward me. You have never forsaken me—not even in my darkest moments. You've always been there to see me through. You move mountains, you make ways straight, you provide, you protect, you forgive, and you heal. You take away my shame and inequities, you break generational curses, you wipe away my tears, you multiply, and you give me hope. You give me peace and beauty for ashes, and you turn my mourning into gladness. You've done so much more, and I don't have enough words to express my gratefulness for who you are and for what you've done. Above all, your presence is everything to me. You have made all things possible. Blessed be your name, Jesus. I praise you, I adore you, and I glorify your holy name.

Since it takes a village to raise a child, I want to acknowledge my parents. Many other family members have invested in my childhood, but there are four of them who I cherish dearly. I am beyond grateful for them. My grandmother, my queen, Vitaly Jean, my dad, Reel Jean, and my two aunties, Mireille Emile and Mimose Lyncee. I love you, Dad, because you are my father and because you were the first one in the entire family who first came to know Jesus Christ as your Lord and Savior. Glory to God that you brought the Gospel to the rest of us. I cannot help but wonder why. Since I was little, I've seen you fighting and surviving the strongest battles that no one else I know would be able to face. I thank God for protecting you and keeping you alive through it all. You have done so much for us, and all we want is to make you a proud father. I pray that God's grace and mercies will continue to see you through.

There aren't enough words to express my gratitude toward Vitaly Jean, Mireille Emile, and Mimose Lyncee. I believe God sent these ladies into my life to help shape me for the type of godly wife and mother who God wanted me to become. You have shaped me and given me my core values and so much, love, compassion, and respect for others. I am extremely grateful for my godmother and aunt, Mimose Lyncee. She has led me and taught me by example. Growing up under your care, I saw how much you love God. Your joy and passion for doing God's work was contagious, and you made it fun and easy for me to follow your lead. I always wanted to be a part of whatever you were doing at church.

When I was around six, my other siblings preferred staying home and playing, but I just wanted to attend choir practice, prayer services, or whatever else was happening at church with you. I am beyond grateful and thank God that you put me on the right path. That is worth more than any gift anyone could ever give me in this lifetime.

At a young adult gathering, the speaker was talking about friendship. She said, "By the time you get older, you'll see that you only need one good friend in your life—or perhaps two friends maximum if you are lucky enough." She was right. I think it is even better when that one good friend is your sister—and you can call yourself blessed if your sister is also a woman who is on fire for God. My one good friend is my sister Rebecca Merzius, and I can call myself blessed to have a good friend who is also passionate about God's kingdom. Your focus is on doing God's work, and many have been blessed tremendously throughout your ministry, preaching, prophesying and your book, *Chosen*. I love and cherish many things about you—like your overachieving personality—but it is even better to know that you're investing your work in God's kingdom.

I want to acknowledge my spiritual father, Senior Pastor and Apostle, Raffoul Najem, for being a true man of God. You preach and teach us nothing but the Word of God. It is a great blessing to be part of a ministry that is all about God's kingdom. Our pastor is pouring into us the things of God in order to get us ready for the Great Commission that Jesus called us to in Matthew 28:19. I love and appreciate Apostle Najem's genuine attitude and personality. Thank you for so tirelessly—along with all the other leaders at CCF Ministries—keeping us in good shape through daily prayer meetings, weekly Bible studies, and Sunday services on livestream media during these hard days where churches have not been able to gather as normal. I praise God for what he is doing throughout you and CCF Ministry, and there is much more to come in Jesus's name!

Last but not least, I am a blessed and happy woman to be the wife of Kenny E. Josselin. Life is good when you marry the man who is in God's divine plan for you. You are a man of God, and you are after God's heart. Thank you for being such a loving, caring husband and a good father to our four children: Henry Josselin, Gabriella Josselin, Juliana Josselin, and Bradley Josselin. We love you more deeply than we can express. I cherish and appreciate how you've always been there with me through all the highs and the lows. Since my teenage years, you have experienced it all with me. I love doing life with you, and I enjoy it even more knowing that God is with us and knowing that we're precious to him:

If God is for us, who can be against us? (Romans 8:31)

Through Jesus, let us conquer the world together for God's kingdom one soul at a time—and all the glory be to God Almighty. Sealed by the blood of the Lamb, Jesus Christ, amen!

PREFACE

What a great privilege and honor to be used by God and to be inspired to write *Godly Wisdom for All*. This book will show you how to apply biblical principles to keep you in good shape when facing adversities. It is intended to help you live a life that is pleasing to God, your Creator. The book is based on the true living Word of God in order to strengthen you spiritually, mentally, and emotionally. After you finish reading this book, I pray that you will be equipped and ready to face any spiritual warfare in your life, in your finances, in your marriage, in your family, in your ministry, in your career, and, most importantly, in your mind.

The enemy is after your soul. Be aware that his main purpose is to keep you in darkness—far away from God—so that you do not make it to heaven. Therefore, he attacks you in nature to cause you to lose your spiritual sights. *Godly Wisdom for All* will help you detect any open doors in your life that may allow access for the devil to come in to steal or destroy the work of God in you. You will learn and understand how every action you take, every word you speak, and every relationship you have has a lot to do with your overall well-being. This book will help you evaluate your motives to make sure they are right and acceptable in God's eyes in order to live an abundant life full of God's love, joy, peace, grace, and favor. Most important, you will have life eternal through Jesus Christ.

May this book give you the clarity that you need to overcome and eliminate confusion, shame, doubt, and fear. May your heart be opened to receiving the fullness of God's love and his forgiveness, which he freely gave to set you free from all bondage and any soul wounds that are affecting your walk with God.

Find a quiet place, read on, and meditate. I pray that you have a new encounter with God. May you receive new spiritual insights and abundant joy of the Lord while you're reading this book! I hope you find clarity, peace of mind, and success in all your ways for God's glory. In Jesus's name! Amen!

PART I
COMPANIONSHIP

CHAPTER 1

Fuel-Less Companions

We all need companionship in order to live joyful and fulfilled lives. Not having companions can cause some people to feel very lonely and depressed. Having companions is very important, but you must learn how to choose them wisely. Don't make the mistake of thinking that companions are a group of friends to hang out with when needed without the intention of achieving anything. You would be better off alone than to be surrounded by "fuel-less" companions who are constantly draining the spiritual life out of you.

How do you recognize if your companions are fuel-less? Simply ask yourself these questions: Are your companions always relying on you for even the simplest things? Are your companions irresponsible? Do they make more withdrawals from you than deposits? Are their minds set on godly things or carnal things? Are they kingdom-minded folks? Are they making progress toward their goals? Have they remained at the same level since the day you met them? You need to know the answers to these questions in order to choose your companions.

Ten virgins were traveling on the road with one purpose: to meet the bridegroom. They all probably had beautified themselves in order to impress the groom. However, some people don't understand that outward appearance is not all there is. Five of the virgins

You have to be courageous and wise to know when to say no to irresponsible people.

were wise, and five were fools (Matthew 25). When you're choosing your companions, you must not be judging them on appearance alone. Otherwise, you might end up traveling with fools who want to depend and rely on your resources, which can be a draining journey.

Those who were foolish took their lamps and took no oil with them, but the wise took oil in their vessels with their lamps. But while the bridegroom was delayed, they all slumbered and slept. "And at midnight a cry was heard: 'Behold, the bridegroom is coming; go out to meet him!' Then all those virgins arose and trimmed their lamps. And the foolish said to the wise, 'Give us some of your oil, for our lamps are going out.' But the wise answered, saying, 'No, lest there should not be enough for us and you; but go rather to those who sell, and buy for yourselves.'" And while they went to buy, the bridegroom came, and those who were ready went in with him to the wedding; and the door was shut. "Afterward the other virgins came also, saying, 'Lord, Lord, open to us!'" But he answered and said, "Assuredly, I say to you, I do not know you." (Matthew 25:3–12)

Fuel-less companions only speak the "give-me" language. They say, "Give me your time, give me your energy, give me your talents, and give me your resources."

The foolish ones said to the wise, "Give us some of your oil; our lamps are going out." (Matthew 25:8)

You have to be courageous and wise to know when to say no to irresponsible people. As a Christian, you are to help those who are in need and not those who are being irresponsible. If you are blessed with the same amount of resources as someone else, and that person chooses not to manage well what God has given to him or her, it is not your responsibility to take care of that person. Don't set yourself on fire to keep someone else warm and expect God to come to deliver you without consulting him first.

Choose your companions wisely. Be aware of the people who always want to use you. Be mindful of the people who want to drag you into their messes. Choose wise, goal-oriented companions who have the mentality to strive for success—no matter how difficult things may appear.

Learn to make kingdom connections. Don't waste time with people who can only see the now. They see the food they are going to eat and the clothes they are going to wear, but they have no goals for the future. The five foolish virgins took only their lamps with them and did not take any oil. The five virgins could not even plan for the next few hours.

These are not the types of companions you want on your journey. While you're talking about strategies and how you're aiming to travel the world to bring the Gospel to those who are lost, the foolish folks are stressing over a basketball game, their nails and hair, or the next movie that's playing in the theater. There's nothing wrong with wanting to do all of these activities, but when they become priorities over the workings of God, it grieves the Holy Spirit because you make no time for God. When you find yourself surrounded with fuel-less companions or people who are slowing you down, you must recognize it. Go in prayer and ask God to send you divine connections with men and women of God who will pour more greatness into you so that you can fulfill your destiny.

CHAPTER 2

The Dream Killers

Most people like to share their dreams, passions, and visions with others because it's human nature. We want to show off who we are, what we have, what makes us different, or what makes us stand out from the crowd. And we expect others to be happy and excited for us when we reveal something dear and special to us. Some of us share our dreams because we need a little bit of motivation from others in order to make our dreams come true.

However, there is also a great danger in opening up and sharing what's in your heart with others, especially when it comes to you being elevated more than them. That could be one of the reasons why God, in all his omniscience, usually chooses not to reveal his plans and promises to us too soon for our own protection.

God gifted Samson with supernatural strength in his mother's womb. His strength was extremely valuable because he protected God's people from their enemies. This special gift of God on Samson's life was supposed to remain a secret. He revealed the secret to his supernatural strength to Delilah—and that cost him his life:

> That he told her all his heart, and said to her, "No razor
> has ever come upon my head, for I have been a Nazirite
> to God from my mother's womb. If I am shaven, then
> my strength will leave me, and I shall become weak,
> and be like any other man." (Judges 16:17)

Pay very close attention to people's reaction when you're sharing your dreams and goals with them. Be sure to watch their reactions, body language, and responses. Their verbal responses may not be what they're actually thinking. Most importantly, you must keep in mind that your battles are more spiritual than you can imagine:

The time to testify will come, but you must wait on the Lord for the right time to do so.

> For we do not wrestle against flesh and blood, but
> against principalities, against powers, against the
> rulers of the darkness of this age, against spiritual
> hosts of wickedness in the heavenly places. (Ephesians
> 6:12)

All the devil is looking for is for you to open your heart to someone who has a little bit of jealousy, unforgiveness, and anger toward you. Once he finds that open door, he will try to use it to his advantage to cause delays. The promise of God to you will surely come to pass:

> God is not a man, that He should lie, Nor a son of man, that He should repent. Has He said, and will He not do? Or has He spoken, and will He not make it good. (Numbers 23:19)

However, something that could have taken you a month to accomplish may end up taking years, simply because you opened your heart and shared the promises that God made to you in secret with the wrong people. Now you have to fight all those demons who are trying to stop you from receiving what's meant for you. Learn to keep your mouth shut while God is working wonders in your life—not everything is meant to be shared right away. The time to testify will come, but you must wait on the Lord so that he can reveal to you when the time is right.

Genesis 37:5–34 is a perfect example of what can happen when you share your dream with others. Joseph, the youngest son of Jacob, shared his dreams with his brothers. When he shared his dreams, his brothers started plotting to kill him because his dreams meant he was going to become a man of power. No older brother would want a younger brother to have dominion over him.

So day after day, they grew jealous and hateful toward him:

> Then they said to one another, "Look, this dreamer is
> coming! Come therefore, let us now kill him and cast
> him into some pit; and we shall say, 'Some wild beast
> has devoured him.' We shall see what will become of
> his dreams!" (Genesis 37:19–20)

The amazing thing about God is that if he gives you a dream, he will make sure that it will come to pass—no matter what the obstacles may be. He will guide and protect you through it all because it's already written in his book. His plan for your life will prevail. However, there are obstacles you can avoid by keeping your mouth shut and waiting on God to know when to speak.

Joseph's brothers changed their plans by doing something they thought would be beneficial to them:

> Judah said to his brothers, "What will we gain if we
> kill our brother and cover up his blood? What profit
> is there if we kill our brother and conceal his blood?
> Come and let us sell him to the Ishmaelites, and let
> not our hand be upon him, for he is our brother and
> our flesh." And his brothers listened. Then Midianite
> traders passed by; so the brothers pulled Joseph up

and lifted him out of the pit, and sold him to the
Ishmaelites for twenty shekels of silver. And they took
Joseph to Egypt. (Genesis 37:26–28)

Joseph's brothers didn't know all the details of Joseph's dreams. If
they only knew that God's plans for Joseph were to become a great
ruler in Egypt, they never would have made the decision to sell him as
a slave to the Egyptians. In the following chapters, we see that Joseph
went through some messed-up things. He was falsely accused, and he
even ended up going to jail in Egypt. However, he prospered through
it all because the hand of God was on him.

In chapter 41, we see that Joseph became in charge of Egypt and
even saved his brothers who had planned to kill him during the big
famine. The dream killers are there to frustrate you and discourage
you. They don't want you to succeed at all. Who could have thought
Joseph's own brothers were plotting against him? The devil has a way
of using those who are the closest to you to harm you. God has all
the power to turn things around and make it work out for you in his
name. So, when you're experiencing warfare, turmoil, and hardship,
don't lose hope. Just remember who gave you the dream in the first
place, God is still on the throne, and it won't be long until he makes
his presence known in your situation. When God gives a dream, he
will make it come to pass.

CHAPTER 3

Who Is in Your Boat?

Where are you heading in this season of your life? Whatever season you are in, it is very important that you take the time to do a companionship assessment to be sure you have the right people with you. Making connections is a very good thing, but making kingdom connections is what really matters. Surround yourself with the people who God intended for you since the beginning of time to help you to fulfill your assignment here on earth. Having a person who is not supposed to be in your life will bring total chaos. You could try everything in your power to make things work, but if you have the wrong person by your side, things will get worse. Therefore, when you notice that you are not progressing in your journey and keep hitting a wall or going in circle, it is necessary to take the time to evaluate the people you are associating with.

The first thing you think about when you read the story of Jonah is that there will be consequences for being disobedient toward God. Running away from what he has assigned you to do is never a good idea. When it comes to God wanting you to fulfill his call on your life, he will make sure you stay alive and well until the work is done. Even after being swallowed by a huge fish, his will, will prevail—regardless of the circumstances.

Do you ever think about the sailors who allowed Jonah to get on their boat? One small decision like welcoming someone into your life can totally ruin everything. As soon as Jonah set foot on the boat, the sailors started experiencing deep trouble (Jonah 1:4). Just because a person is a minister does not mean you should allow them to partake in your journey without first consulting God.

Many people have experienced hardship while doing ministry. One simple decision can cause a lot frustration, loss, pain, tears, and even delay along the way. Well, glory be to God! He is a God of second chances, and he allows us to begin again. The

Always keep in mind anyone who chooses to live in disobedience with God does not fit to be part of your journey.

next time around, you'll be wiser—and you will be in sync with the Holy Spirit to avoid trouble.

God might send a storm into your life to cleanse and remove whoever or whatever is not supposed to be there.

> But the Lord sent out a great wind on the sea, and there was a mighty tempest on the sea, so that the ship was about to be broken up. (Jonah 1:4)

Jonah did not belong in the ship. When you find yourself in the darkest moments of your life—after you've tried everything else—don't get discouraged or give up. Instead, take a moment to think things through and ask yourself if someone or something you have allowed into your life is causing you to be in a dark place. If it is difficult to identify if there's a Jonah in your life, here is what you need to know:

1. Jonah is disobedient to God.
2. Jonah is using you.
3. Jonah will not pray with you.
4. Jonah has his own agenda.
5. Jonah sleeps while you are in deep trouble.

> So the captain came to him, and said to him, "What do you mean, sleeper? Arise, call on your God; perhaps your God will consider us, so that we may not perish." (Jonah 1:6)

Once you have identified the Jonah in your life, do what the sailors did to Jonah.

> So they picked up Jonah and threw him into the sea,
> and the sea ceased from its raging. (Jonah 1:15)

Waste no time—and do not make excuses—in getting him off your boat because the longer you keep Jonas around, the more hardship you'll experience. Anyone who chooses to live in disobedience with God is not fit to be part of your journey. This person will only bring frustration, confusion, delay, and chaos to your life.

CHAPTER 4

Ear Gate Protection

We often hear a lot of teaching about the heart, but we don't nearly as much about the ear gate. The ear gate is probably one of the most important things, and you must take all necessary precautions and actions to protect it by being fully aware of what you're allowing to enter so you do not become spiritually deaf.

When was the last time you heard from God without consulting a minister to give you a word concerning your situation? There is absolutely nothing wrong with consulting a prophet to receive a word from the Lord or asking for others to pray for you and with you. However, there comes a time when you'll need to keep pressing on all by yourself through prayer and fasting to get closer to God until your spirit is synchronized with the Holy Spirit so that he can speak to you directly. If or when God decides to use a prophet to minister to you, it will just be a confirmation or a reminder of what God has already spoken to you. If you are receiving a revelation from a prophet, you should be able to discern if it's coming from God through the Holy Spirit that is in you also because there is only one Spirit:

> Beloved, do not believe every spirit, but test the spirits,
> whether they are of God; because many false prophets
> have gone out into the world. (1 John 4:1)

Under the law, it was impossible for anyone to access God's presence in the holy of holies. Only the high priest was granted access to enter the holy of holies once a year on the day of atonement by following specific instructions to offer up a sacrifice on behalf of the people, and there was still a chance that the high priest would not make it out alive if he had not followed all the God-given instructions. Can you imagine how that period was for God's people?

> Now the Lord spoke to Moses after the death of the
> two sons of Aaron, when they offered profane fire
> before the Lord, and died; and the Lord said to Moses:
> "Tell Aaron your brother not to come at just any time
> into the Holy Place inside the veil, before the mercy
> seat which is on the ark, lest he die; for I will appear
> in the cloud above the mercy seat." (Leviticus 16:1–2)

Glory and honor be to our God Almighty for his everlasting love toward us and that He sent his only begotten Son, Jesus Christ, to offer up his body as the perfect sacrifice for our sins. The thick veil that used to prevent access to anyone from entering the holy of holies inside the tabernacle was torn from top to bottom.

> Now we all have been granted access, through Jesus Christ to the throne of grace to speak, hear from God and remain alive, what a Grace, and blessed assurance! (Matthew 27:51)

> Let us therefore come boldly to the throne of grace, that we may obtain mercy and find grace to help in time of need. (Hebrews 4:16)

Who or what do you give your ears to?

> For the time will come when they will not endure sound doctrine; but after their own lusts shall they heap to themselves teachers, having itching ears; And they shall turn away their ears from the truth, and shall be turned unto fables. (2 Timothy 4:3–4)

Are you too busy listening to the lies from the enemy: ungodly music, gossiping spirits, and the negative noise of social media? Have you truly been born again? If you are born again, your ears should become so sensitive to the point where you should immediately feel uncomfortable if you hear negativity. Ungodliness and wickedness should not sit well with you if you are a child of God.

If you say you are a born-again Christian, why are you still struggle with protecting your ear gate? Don't you think the devil knows if you still give ears to gossip or if you're still listening to and dancing to worldly music that is filled with profane language because you like the sound of it? Most people would not listen to or dance to bad music that is filled with profane language. The way you get delivered is by praying and asking God to fill you up with his love until there is no more room for ungodliness:

> Do not love the world or the things in the world. If
> anyone loves the world, the love of the Father is not
> in him. (1 John 2:15)

The Word of God clearly says the love of God is not in a person if they love worldly things. After you ask God to fill you up with his love, do not stop there. You need engage yourself by listening to sound doctrine, studying the Word of God, and listening to godly music.

> So then faith comes by hearing, and hearing by the
> word of God. (Romans 10:17)

There are countless scriptures about how important it is to give ears to wisdom, especially in the book of Proverbs, because God knows how the enemy can turn your life upside down with fear, doubt, anxiety, depression, lack of self-control, and taking your peace of mind if you don't protect your ear gate.

> My son, if you receive my words, And treasure my commands within you, So that you incline your ear to wisdom, And apply your heart to understanding; Yes, if you cry out for discernment, and lift up your voice for understanding, If you seek her as silver, and search for her as for hidden treasures; then you will understand the fear of the Lord, and find the knowledge of God. For the Lord gives wisdom; From His mouth come knowledge and understanding; He stores up sound wisdom for the upright; He is a shield to those who walk uprightly; He guards the paths of justice, and preserves the way of His saints. Then you will understand righteousness and justice, equity and every good path. When wisdom enters your heart, and knowledge is pleasant to your soul. (Proverbs 2:1–10)

CHAPTER 5

Temporary People

Everybody likes sunshine! When everything is nice and bright in your life, who would not want to be around you? You are healthy, you have a great career, your bills are paid on time, there's food on the table, your children are healthy, you're doing great, you have money saved up in the bank, your spouse is doing wonderful, your marriage is flourishing, you have extra to give to the poor, and everything is blooming. You have such a positive energy that the smile on your face and the joy in your heart brighten someone's else day. Your positive spirit makes everything around you look beautiful. The fact of the matter is that all of us will experience the highs and the lows, and it is important to know the difference between the people who will stick by your side no matter the circumstances—and whether you are happy or sad—and there usually aren't many.

Beware of temporary people. When things are going wrong in your life, they are the first to talk badly and spread rumors about you. They are the ones to quickly judge you, blame you, and say how you deserve what's happening to you. When you need someone to comfort you, these people will be bad-mouthing you instead. They may say, "You lost your job because you're not a good employee," "Your children are disobedient because you are not a good parent," or "Your marriage is failing because you're not a loving spouse."

> *Pay close attention to how people treat you and if they are quick to judge you when you are experiencing difficult times.*

God allowed Satan to take away everything that Job had possessed to prove to him that Job was a righteous man and he would never curse God, however, when he lost everything his friends were quick to blame and judge him. His friend Eliphaz said to him "Remember now, who ever perished being innocent? Or where were the upright ever cut off? Even as I have seen, those who plow iniquity and sow trouble reap the same." (Job 8:20)

His friend Zophar said "If iniquity were in your hand, and you put it far away, and would not let wickedness dwell in your tents; then surely you could lift up your face without spot; yes, you could be steadfast, and not fear; because you would forget your misery, and remember it as waters that have passed away, and your life would be brighter than noonday. Though you were dark, you would be like the morning." (Job 11:14–17)

Not one of Job's friends suggested praying with him or giving him hope that the same God who blessed him before would bless him again and restore his health. They sat with Job and told him how he was being punished by God for his iniquity.

Pay close attention to how people treat you and if they are quick to judge you when you are experiencing difficult times. You need to know that most people that hang out with when things are rosy are not going to be there for you when you're in deep trouble, so to save yourself from being disappointed, always remember not to put your expectation too high on temporary people.

CHAPTER 6

The Beloved Friend

Do you have a beloved friend in your life? If not, it is time to pray God to send you one. A beloved friend is a friend who you can have a heart-to-heart conversation with without any fear and with total confidence that this person will never turn against you or betray you when times get rough.

This type of friendship is mutual. You're a blessed person if you have a genuine friend in your life. How do you recognize if you have a beloved friend in your life? This friend is someone you can rely on and even trust with your life. Never take this friend for granted because such a friend is not easy to find.

Have you ever had an important conversation with someone and asked them not to tell anyone else? Well, if you're 100 percent sure that you are talking to your beloved friend, you don't even have to mention not telling anyone else about the conversation because what's dear to you is dear to your friend and what's a secret to you will forever remain a secret to them as well.

Be sure to give the friendship the test of time because anything that is valuable takes time. Keep your eyes open because not every person who says they have your best interests in mind is your confidant. Just because someone says they like you doesn't make them your beloved friend. Many

True friendship is built on genuine love, respect, loyalty, transparency,and confidentiality.

people get hurt after opening up too quickly, and they end up being disappointed.

The twelve disciples were always with Jesus, but one of the disciples always knew everything before the others knew. Apostle John was referred to several times in the Bible as "the disciple whom Jesus loved."

At their gatherings, John would sit closer to Jesus, and his head would be on Jesus chest, which symbolizes being closer to Jesus's heart. Let this be an example to you that not everyone in your life needs to be that close to your heart. One good friend is all you need. If Jesus had only chosen one out of the twelve, why do you think it would be wise to have more than one friend who is close to your heart?

Jesus trusted John so much that before Jesus died, he showed us which disciples he trusted to take care of his loved ones:

> Now there stood by the cross of Jesus His mother, and His mother's sister, Mary the wife of Clopas, and Mary Magdalene. When Jesus therefore saw His mother, and the disciple whom He loved standing by, He said to His mother, "Woman, behold your son!" (John 19:25–26)

I am not sure where the rest of the disciples were at Jesus's Crucifixion, but scripture documented that apostle John was standing by the cross along with Jesus's mother. Out of all the disciples, he chose John to be a son to Mary because he was that beloved disciple to Jesus.

Apostle John demonstrates the characteristics of a truly beloved friend. A beloved friend will care for you, your family, and your business as if they were their own. If anything bad were to happen, this person would be there for you—like no one else would—without expecting anything in return.

CHAPTER 7

Managing Popularity

In today's world, everybody wants to be popular. Many people are extremely thirsty for fame and glory. With the help of social media, including Facebook, YouTube, Twitter, and Instagram, anyone can become famous. Many people use social media in a malicious way, but many people with great intentions are using the web to make a tremendous difference in the lives of others.

As the popularity of social media is rising, so is the suicidal rate—even among Christians. According to CDC's Morbidity and Mortality Weekly Report Centers for Disease Control and Prevention research done by Alyson Hurt/NPR, suicide rates have increased in nearly every state over the past two decades, and half of the states have seen suicide rates go up more than 30 percent.

Are you popular, influential, or charismatic? Do you often find that people gravitate toward you, searching for something that will satisfy them emotionally, mentally, spiritually, physically, or financially? Maybe you are highly gifted and talented. If you answer yes to any of these questions, you will need to learn quickly how to deal with the crowd in order to keep your life balance. If not, the fame can become destructive and eventually ruin your life.

There is nothing wrong with being famous, and God never intended for Christians to be infamous or unremarkable. Jesus was popular, and he made it clear that for us to follow his footsteps, we must become popular for spiritual reasons and not for carnal reasons. Jesus gave us a mission statement:

> Go therefore and make disciples of all nations, baptizing them in the name of the Father and of the Son and of the Holy Spirit. (Matthew 28:19)

Jesus called us to go to nations. How can this mission be accomplished if we only stay in our local churches every Sunday—privately—and do not share what we know about Jesus with our next-door neighbors and coworkers? Christianity is not a title; it is a lifestyle, and we are on a mission to bring people to God.

Learn to spend some quality time alone, away from the noise, go before God in prayer, and ask him to humble you to never become prideful.

If you know a little bit about Jesus, you'll understand why hanging out with the crowd does not necessarily mean hanging out with friends. That's where many people get trapped. They rely on the crowd as their fuel to keep them going, and the more enchantments they receive, the more they require in order to survive. When fame becomes an idol, it automatically becomes an open door that the devil can use at any given point in time.

Jesus was omniscient and knew exactly what the crowd was about. He could see everyone's hearts and hear everyone's thoughts. Most of the time, he could only find one person in the crowd who was actually seeking after him truthfully. An example would be the woman with the blood condition. If you had the spiritual gift of hearing everyone's thoughts and seeing everyone's hearts, you would understand why Jesus never depended on the crowd's enchantments.

Jesus knew whether the people following him were real or fake. He knew who was following him because they needed to be fed. He knew who needed to be healed. He knew who came to be entertained and see miracles signs and wonders. That explains why most people who have the gift of seeing and discerning of spirits are usually loners who don't have too many friends. Jesus loved his followers, but he never let their cheering and praises go above his head. The same crowd that applauded him for doing the miracles shouted, "Crucify him!"

> Then he said to them the third time, "Why, what evil has He done? I have found no reason for death in Him. I will therefore chastise Him and let Him go." But they were insistent, demanding with loud voices that He be crucified. And the voices of these men and of the chief priests prevailed. So Pilate gave sentence that it should be as they requested. (Luke 23:22–24)

You may have reached a point in your life where you're asking yourself where they are. You might have thought the people you put all your hopes and trust in would always be there for you. You invested so much of your time and energy, but now you feel like you've got no one to count on. Where is one voice when you need to hear it the most? And where is one shoulder to lean on when you feel all alone? When reality knocks on your door, you realize that having a crowd means nothing at all.

The worst thing you can do is become angry, bitter, or resentful. The crowds don't really care much about you and how you feel. Some people have committed suicide when they lost the popularity and fame they used to have. They placed their self-worth in the enchantments of others, became puffed up by pride, and took the glory that was meant to be given to God for themselves.

Although Jesus was popular, he avoided publicity and lived a simple and quiet life. Learn to spend some quality time alone, away from the noise, go before God in prayer, and ask him to humble you to never become prideful. After Jesus completed a miracle, he would disappear from the crowd in order to get replenished. Learn to love who you are as a person—and not just what you do. It is medicine to your soul, and you will never feel alone or need the approval of others to survive.

> And when he had sent the multitudes away, he went up
> into a mountain apart to pray and when the evening
> came, he was there alone. (Matthew 14:23)

PART II

KINGDOM MINDED

CHAPTER 8

Dreams on Standby

Do you feel frustrated or impatient about the call of God on your life? You have been called and anointed to become something greater than you could ever imagine, but you're looking at things with your natural eyes and asking how in the world this is ever going to happen. Based on your current situation, you would not even dare to tell anyone about all the promises that God made to you because it would be laughable. You try not focus too much on these thoughts because they are too big for your mind to comprehend. How could a young shepherd with no skills, training, or qualification ever become the king of a great nation?

> *God has a special way of shocking everyone who has been looking down on you.*

But God has chosen the foolish things of the world to put to shame the wise, and God has chosen the weak things of the world to put to shame the things which are mighty; and the base things of the world and the things which are despised God has chosen, and the things which are not, to bring to nothing the things that are, that no flesh should glory in His presence. (1 Corinthians 1:27–29)

You are probably 100 percent right that there is nothing about you that resembles a palace or is fit to wear a crown. You are trying to live your regular life, living from paycheck to paycheck, struggling to keep up with the bills, and pretending not to bother with the anointed oil that was poured over your head and the powerful words deliverance that were spoken to you by the ministers of God. However, these words keep replaying in your mind, and you keep receiving confirmation after confirmation from visions and dreams like an alarm clock that keeps reminding you that the time will eventually come to be lifted up. You will soon be placed in a high position, and the name of God will be glorified through you. You may think you're not fit for it, and your friends might not think you're fit for it. Your family definitely knows you're not fit for it because they know where you came from. They know all about the good, the bad, and the ugly situations you've been through. They know how many times you've messed up, and they know about your present struggles.

God has a special way of shocking you—and everyone who has been looking down on you. He has a way of surprising everyone who thought you would never amount to anything. God will keep your enemies alive so they can witness God's promises being fulfilled. He will raise you up right before their eyes, above their heads, and they will look up at you.

> He raises the poor from the dust and lifts the beggar from the ash heap, to set them among princes and make them inherit the throne of glory. (1 Samuel 2:8)

For the pillars of the earth are the Lord's, and he has set the world upon them.

Are you a royal on standby? Have you received God's call for your life? If you're clueless and don't know how to answer this question, it simply means that you need to get connected to God. The Creator of the universe created everything with a unique purpose. The greatest architect placed a huge ball of fire called the sun at a perfect distance from the earth, and it gives us light and warmth. It would be impossible to live without it. He orders it to rise every day but never come too close; otherwise, we would all perish.

God can speak to the oceans, order a great flood to cover the whole earth, and wipe out everything that moves and everything that exists in an instant. However, he also saved Noah's family since he had found them worthy enough to live (Genesis 6:9–9:1). That's the God you need to pray to and find out why on earth you exist. With all the knowledge, techniques, software, and top-of-the-line materials that humans possess, we cannot come close to the magnificent simplicity of God. He picked up some dust, made man in his own image, breathed into his nostril, gave him life, a body, a spirit, and a soul, and multiplied his creation. He uttered that a man's seed meets a woman's womb to create another human. That's the Almighty God!

When you feel a void on the inside and are not satisfied, avoid going to other people to find the answers to your problems. They may take your money and charge you countless fees for their advice and services, but they cannot fill the void you're feeling inside.

This void or emptiness is God's way of guiding humankind back to our Creator. Do not waste time creating your own religion or statues or linking up with other evil spiritual forces to obtain the power to make it through life. You might find temporary satisfaction—and you may even seem to be content on the outside—but deep inside, you know, the devil knows, and God knows you're lonely and empty.

Don't fill your life up with temporary pleasures to mask the void. The right thing to do is declutter your life. God created you and gave you with free will to decide whether you prefer to live your life with him or without him. You have to be willing to invite Jesus—who died on the cross for our sins—to come into your life and be your Lord and Savior to fill the gap. Once you allow him to come into your life, he will begin to reveal his divine plans and divine purpose for your life.

Right now, you may have a false point of view about yourself because your point of view has been corrupted. With so many things that you've been through in life, you start to look at yourself in the same way others do. Since you were born, you have been given labels based on your features, strengths, intellect, attitude, personality, flaws, and nationality. The list goes on and on, and because of these earthly labels, you have lost your true identity.

Don't let life pass you by as you live a lie that the world has placed on you. Do not allow yourself to become miserable, stressful, unfulfilled, and unhappy because you are unaware of who God says you are. Allow God to show you who you really are so that you can live the meaningful life that God purposely designed for you at the beginning of time. Let him show you exactly what you are made of. Allow God to reveal your real strength. That strength is not based on successful experiences; it is based on what he placed inside of you in order to thrive. Allow him you to show you your weaknesses. They are not based on your failures; they are based on the limitations he placed inside you to protect you from going too far beyond your limits.

David was labeled as the shepherd boy and based on the physical attributes of his brothers, it seems like his brothers may have been more physically appealing than he was. The time came when God needed to choose a king to replace King Saul because he was living in disobedience to God. God sent the prophet Samuel to Jesse's house to choose and anoint a king among his sons. Jesse set up the event or presentation with all his sons, but David—the youngest—was out taking care of his father's sheep.

When the time comes for you to receive your blessing—no matter how strongly qualified others may appear to be in comparison to you— rest assured that God never makes mistakes or accidents. He will not give what's yours to someone else just because you're absent. What is meant for you will always and forever remain yours. No matter how much you've been excluded from the pack, cut off, left off the list, denied access, not invited, put in a corner, or left in exile, the day will not end until you receive what's yours. David was not even considered by his own father to be the king, but God spoke to Samuel about David's brother:

> But the Lord said to Samuel, "Do not look at his appearance or at his physical stature, because I have refused him. For the Lord does not see as man sees; for man looks at the outward appearance, but the Lord looks at the heart." (1 Samuel 16:7)

Your heavenly Father sees your heart. He knows how much you love him and have been faithful with little, and he will bless you with much more. You don't need to seek praise or rely on others to get promoted. Your heavenly Father knows you inside out, and he takes all your hard work and effort into consideration, and his reward is greater and better than what others can give you.

You may think you are at the lowest point of your life because you are taking care of sheep all day long. All you hear is baa, baa, baa, but everyone else seems to be doing big things and interesting things. You don't even know how to interact with them because you don't have anything interesting to talk about.

Although you are the future king or queen, you do not even dare to mention it because it would be laughable for that to come out of the mouth of someone who only has experience with sheep. As the years go by, you start to lose faith. You start to question the day you were anointed and chosen to be a king or queen. Nothing seems to be different. You're still watching after the sheep, and the people who knew about the promise God made to you start to wonder what's taking you so long. They might even think that God has forgotten about you. Be encouraged! *You're a royal on standby.*

God loves you too much to put you out before your time! The wisest thing to do is to remain on standby until God releases you. In the meantime, continue to watch over the sheep without complaining because the place where God is getting ready to take you, you are going to need more than just a few years of sheep training to make it through successfully.

The sheep represented the people of Israel due to their lack of understanding and rebellion against God. The Israelites were disobedient and ungrateful, and at times, they would worship foreign gods even though they had seen God's wonders and how he always delivered them from their enemies. David did not despise his occupation as a shepherd. He was such a good shepherd that he would kill lions and bears to protect the sheep.

> But David said to Saul, "Your servant used to keep his father's sheep, and when a lion or a bear came and took a lamb out of the flock, I went out after it and struck it, and delivered the lamb from its mouth; and when it arose against me, I caught it by its beard, and struck and killed it. Your servant has killed both lion and bear; and this uncircumcised Philistine will be like one of them, seeing he has defied the armies of the living God." (1 Samuel 17:34–36)

In order for King David to become the greatest in Israel and lead Israel according to God's principles, he needed to learn how to be a great shepherd. What is God teaching you in this season of your life? Do not try to rush the process because God is preparing you for something greater. In due time, you will be transitioned from being a shepherd to a king or queen. Be patient and remain faithful in your current situation.

CHAPTER 9

Meaningful Associations

When God is getting ready to use you to do greater works in his kingdom, you will begin to see a major shift happening in your life. It will seem as if your world is turning upside down, but that's God's way of letting you know it's time to move out of your comfort zone and trust him to step in to take control of your life. What God is about to do in your life is far beyond your imagination. What's taking place is not in the natural realm. It is supernatural, and you will notice things shifting. You will have no option but to be still and let God operate in your life. You might as well say, "Here I am, God. I promise not to interfere. Just give me the courage to be patient, the wisdom to be obedient, and the intelligence to get out of the box to meet new people—mighty men and women of God who are giants in your kingdom and can influence me in a spiritual way."

To really focus on God's kingdom, you'll need to be surrounded by people who are doing God's will and who are mature enough and willing to help strengthen you along the way. Jesus did not call the disciples to walk alone; he called them as a group. Throughout the New Testament, we learn how the disciples used to always gather to spend time together praying, eating, and ministering. The disciples probably had regular lives before they started to follow Jesus. They probably had regular jobs, hobbies, and friends, but everything changed when they met Jesus. They left everything behind and lived their lives with a new purpose: to enrich God's kingdom.

> And Jesus, walking by the Sea of Galilee, saw two brothers, Simon called Peter, and Andrew his brother, casting a net into the sea; for they were fishermen. Then He said to them, "Follow Me, and I will make you fishers of men." They immediately left their nets and followed Him. (Matthew 4:18–20)

Once you've decided to be all about God's kingdom, your old non-Christian friends probably will not join you in the race. Do not worry about this because God is omniscient. He knows who will remain with you and who will leave. Christian friends with

God is a God of order, and he will not dwell in a place where there is disorder.

good intentions might want to remain close, but God can see that they might hinder your walk with him. God will allow certain situations to take place to make it easier for you to separate yourself and focus on what God has called you to do.

In the body of Christ, we all have different functions. If God calls you to be the right leg, then you need to find out who in the body is called to be the left leg. You must get together so the body of Christ can stand up straight, walk, and run if it needs to. This way, there will be no conflicts. It is not that you have anything against another sister or brother who's called to be the mouth or the head, but you need get in place so the body of Christ can function properly.

> There are diversities of gifts, but the same Spirit. There are differences of ministries, but the same Lord. And there are diversities of activities, but it is the same God who works all in all. (1 Corinthians 12:4–6)

There are so many ministries that are not functioning right. It's not because they are not called by God to do the work of his kingdom; it's because things are not in order. The leg wants to be the head, and the head wants to be the hands. In that fashion, they create chaos among themselves to the point that even the ungodly folks that are watching can't take the church seriously . God is a God of order, and he will not dwell in a place where there is disorder.

For as we have many members in one body, but all the members do not have the same function, so we, being many, are one body in Christ, and individually members of one another. (Romans 12:4–5)

When God chose you, he had already prepared a group of godly, kingdom-minded people to mentor you along the way. He will provide you with all you need—spiritual friends, parents, family, and spiritual provisions—to meet your needs. That's how great God is! Therefore, be obedient and follow him. If he says move, get up and leave. If he says be still, remain still.

Paul hated and persecuted Christians. When he had an encounter with Jesus, the Lord did not leave him clueless to figure out things on his own. God spoke with Ananias in a vision and gave him an assignment to go pray with Paul. Paul had dealt very harshly with the Christians. He had beaten, jailed, and killed many Christians. Many of them probably wanted God to deal harshly with Paul in return. Despite everything he had done, God told Ananias, one of the disciples, to go pray with Paul to restore his eyesight:

Then Ananias answered, "Lord, I have heard from many about this man, how much harm he has done to Your saints in Jerusalem. And here he has authority from the chief priests to bind all who call on Your name." But the Lord said to him, "Go, for he is a chosen vessel of Mine to bear My name before Gentiles, kings, and the children of Israel. For I will show him how many things he must suffer for My name's sake." And Ananias went his way and entered the house; and laying his hands on him he said, "Brother Saul, the Lord Jesus, who appeared to you on the road as you came, has sent me that you may receive your sight and be filled with the Holy Spirit." Immediately there fell from his eyes something like scales, and he received his sight at once; and he arose and was baptized. So when he had received food, he was strengthened. Then Saul spent some days with the disciples at Damascus. (Acts 9:13–19)

Even if you were the worst person on the face of the earth, when you come to Jesus, he will assign people to bless you, pray for you, and be there for you. God is a merciful God. His love is everlasting, and his grace overflows. Don't worry about your old reputation. Even if others want to use it to bring you down, God will use it to set them free. The uglier the mess, the more powerful the message. God has a way of turning broken things into priceless masterpieces. Paul was one of the greatest apostles who ever lived:

I have fought the good fight, I have finished the race, I have kept the faith. Henceforth there is laid up for me the crown of righteousness, which the Lord, the righteous judge, will award to me on that Day, and not only to me but also to all who have loved his appearing. (2 Timothy 4:7–8)

As Jim George said, "It's not how you start that's important—but how you finish!"

CHAPTER 10

Facing the Unknown

One of the hardest things in life is learning how to let go of things that no longer help us get better. It is difficult to leave behind the things and the people we are accustomed to because we are fearful of the unknown.

Dwelling in a place when God is calling you to leave is one of the most dangerous things you can do to yourself and your loved ones. Perhaps you are staying for the sake of your own comfort or for selfish reasons—or maybe it's a lack of faith. It takes faith to move forward and let God guide you to the place where he has promised to take you. In life, you must learn not to allow yourself to get too comfortable and become complacent. Do not become too attached to things and people or let them become your idols. When you allow people and things to become your idols, they will kill you spiritually. How good can you be physically if you are dead spiritually?

Here's a perfect example from the Bible about how to leave a place that no longer serves you:

> Now Jacob heard the words of Laban's sons, saying, "Jacob has taken away all that was our father's, and from what was our father's he has acquired all this wealth." And Jacob saw the countenance of Laban, and indeed it was not favorable toward him as before. Then the Lord said to Jacob, "Return to the land of your fathers and to your family, and I will be with you." (Genesis 31:1–3)

If you have been in a place for a very long time and have committed your time, love, and passion to serve, you've done the best you can. If you have gone above and beyond in everything you do, you will end up prospering because God will honor your faithfulness to the work you do.

There is no way you can possibly live life to the fullest when you are living outside of the will of God.

When you start getting blessed, pay close attention to the attitudes of the people around you. Some people can only hold you while you are in the pit, but as soon as things start turning in your favor, their attitudes will change drastically. You will experience jealousy, hatred, betrayal, and loneliness, but none of these will stop you from getting blessed. You will be prospering during the chaos, which can make it difficult to leave.

How do you know if it is time to leave and say goodbye? Genesis 31:3 holds the answer:

> Then the Lord said to Jacob, "Go back to the land of your fathers and to your relatives, and I will be with you."

All you need to know is that God is telling you to leave—and that he promises to be with you in your departure. Even if God calls you to leave the land that seems to be the richest land in the world to go live in an inhabitable desert, you must remember that he has a divine plan for you to prosper there. If you choose to stay in a place that you think is best for you, you might end up losing everything because your plans are not in sync with God's plans—and you're living in disobedience.

In most cases, God calls people to start fresh in a place they've never heard of before—just like he did with Abraham:

> Now the Lord had said to Abram: "Get out of your country, from your family and from your father's house, to a land that I will show you." (Genesis 12:1)

However, Jacob's experience with God was different. God told him to go back to the land of his father. You can't focus on what God is doing with other people to make your decisions. You have to get into God's plans to find out exactly what he wants to do with you. It was not an easy decision for Jacob to go back to his father's house after lied to him. Jacob had a lot of fear knowing that everyone would be against him. Therefore, going back to his father's land would have been the last thing on his mind. In would have been easier for Jacob to go to a new land, start fresh, and face the unknown instead of facing his brother Esau—who had been planning to kill him for stealing his birthright and blessings:

> Then Jacob put his children and his wives on camels, and he drove all his livestock ahead of him, along with all the goods he had accumulated in Paddan Aram, to go to his father Isaac in the land of Canaan. (Genesis 31:17)

There is no way you can possibly live life to the fullest when you are living outside the will of God. If you want to know the purpose behind your existence, you're going to need to get on the same page with God. Otherwise, you will miss out on the greater purpose for your life. On his way back to his father's house, Jacob had the greatest encounter with God:

And He said, "Let Me go, for the day breaks." But he said, "I will not let You go unless You bless me!" So He said to him, "What is your name?" He said, "Jacob." And He said, "Your name shall no longer be called Jacob, but Israel; for you have struggled with God and with men and have prevailed." Then Jacob asked, saying, "Tell me Your name, I pray." And He said, "Why is it that you ask about My name?" And He blessed him there. So Jacob called the name of the place Peniel: "For I have seen God face to face, and my life is preserved." the place Peniel saying, "It is because I saw God face to face, and yet my life was spared." (Genesis 32:26–30)

Jacob's obedience led to the greatest blessing. This time around, the blessings he had received were not material things. It was a spiritual, supernatural blessing, which is the type of blessing that you can only receive when you obey God, when you seek God's face and not his hands. Through him, the nation of Israel was birthed. God also turned around the fear he had for his brother Esau:

But Esau ran to meet him, and embraced him, and fell on his neck and kissed him, and they wept. (Genesis 33:4)

CHAPTER 11

Life Assignment

Life is a precious gift from God, and the fact that you are alive today makes you a winner. Just think about how many other people could have been born in your place. Always remember that you were born a winner! Do not let the devil tell you otherwise. You were chosen by God to exist here on earth because he has unique purpose and assignment for your life. You are more than your ethnicity, social class, or career. To understand your kingdom assignment, you need to first know Jesus as your personal Savior by giving your life to Christ to save your soul and being born again, which will guarantee your life eternal in heaven:

> Jesus answered and said to him, "Most assuredly, I
> say to you, unless one is born again, he cannot see the
> kingdom of God." (John 3:3)

Many people are living without knowing their true purpose in life because they have not yet made the decision to belong to God's kingdom. Jesus made it clear that you will not see the kingdom of God if you are not born again. To get into some high places on earth, you need to be registered. In most cases, you would be charged a fee for the registration, and without a valid verification, your access would be denied.

To understand the true meaning of kingdom assignment, you must be able to take your focus off of carnal things.

Who on earth with their sinful nature could possibly enter God's most luminous glorious presence and stand before him without being born again? No one!

> For You are not a God who takes pleasure in wickedness, Nor shall evil dwell with You. (Psalm 5:4)

God is so merciful. He did not allow us to pay the high price of crucifixion in order to be born again to belong in his kingdom. He did not ask us to pay a certain amount of money to receive salvation. Instead, he sent Jesus Christ his only begotten Son blameless to die on the cross for our sins.

> For by grace you have been saved through faith; and that not of yourselves, it is the gift of God;

not because of works, so that no one may boast.
(Ephesians 2:8–9)

Since Jesus taught us in order to see God's kingdom, we must be saved. If you truly belong to God, it should not be a puzzle to find out what your life assignment is. Once you have accepted Jesus Christ as your Lord and Savior, you will be made new:

Therefore, if anyone is in Christ, he is a new creation; old things have passed away; behold, all things have become new. (2 Corinthians 5:17)

The Holy Spirit will come and live inside of you like a brand-new hard drive that will help you function properly. The Holy Spirit will govern your life to make sure your life is not wasted. Your soul will be untouchable by the devil, and your place in heaven will be guaranteed after death. The Holy Spirit will direct you in which way you should go, what to do, and when to act so that you can live your life to the fullest:

But the manifestation of the Spirit is given to each one for the profit of all: for to one is given the Word of wisdom through the Spirit, to another the Word of knowledge through the same Spirit, to another faith by the same Spirit, to another gifts of healings by the same Spirit, to another the working of miracles, to another prophecy, to another discerning of spirits, to another different kinds of tongues, to another the interpretation of tongues. But one and the same Spirit works all these things, distributing to each one individually as He wills. (1 Corinthians 12:7–11)

But the fruit of the Spirit is love, joy, peace, longsuffering, kindness, goodness, faithfulness, gentleness, self-control. Against such there is no law. (Galatians 5:22–23)

You can't say you are saved without having the evidence that you possessed some of the fruits and gifts of the Holy Spirit because the fruits and gifts of the Holy Spirit are the attributes that set you apart from the carnal and the ungodly people of this world. Moreover, they are the requirements and qualifications that enable you to accomplish your life assignment in accordance with God's plan for your life. How can you say you're called to be an evangelist without having the fruits of love, kindness, peace, and gentleness to the ones who do not know Jesus and need to hear about the love of God? How can you say you are called to be a prophet or apostle without having the fruits of the spirit such as self-control, goodness, and faithfulness to live a life that is pleasing to God so that unbelievers can see the glory of God through you?

The Word of God says clearly that you will know them by their fruits:

> Beware of false prophets, who come to you in sheep's clothing, but inwardly they are ravenous wolves. You will know them by their fruits. Do men gather grapes from thornbushes or figs from thistles? Even so, every good tree bears good fruit, but a bad tree bears bad fruit. A good tree cannot bear bad fruit, nor can a bad tree bear good fruit. Every tree that does not bear good fruit is cut down and thrown into the fire. Therefore by their fruits you will know them. (Matthew 7:15–20)

To understand the true meaning of your kingdom assignment, you must be able to take your focus off of the carnal things of this world and focus on the eternal being God created you to be. Do you ever ask yourself why on earth are you here? Do you ever have a desire to do something extraordinary? The passion that is burning inside you is what makes you who you are. It makes you different from everyone else. Even if it looks like someone else is doing something similar, don't be discouraged or think that your ideas, creativity, and passion are not as valuable because it has already been projected by someone else. Take the initiative to birth it out because yours will be different. Just think about a room filled with pregnant mothers; they will all be giving birth to their babies, but each baby will be different.

Do not take lightly the call of God over your life. In the end, we will all have to stand before God to give an account of what we've done with the life, gifts, and talents he gave us. We will not be able to give excuses because God knows it all. Your pastor, your spouse, your children, and your friends may believe your excuses, but God knows it all. He is omniscient, and everything is naked before him. Therefore, do your kingdom assignment and make it your priority because you'll have to answer for yourself.

Christianity is not just a religion; it is a personal relationship with God. Together, we walk in obedience, which will bring light to the world:

> You are the light of the world. A city that is set on a hill cannot be hidden. Nor do they light a lamp and put it under a basket, but on a lampstand, and it gives light to all who are in the house. Let your light so shine before men, that they may see your good works and glorify your Father in heaven. (Matthew 5:14–16)

CHAPTER 12

Watch Your Heart

You have answered the call of God on your life, and the time has come to be out in the field to preach, teach, prophesy, evangelize, and operate miracles, signs, and wonders. In whatever God calls you to do, remember that your heart posture before God is what matters. It doesn't matter how well you can minister if your heart is not pleasing to God. Everybody may be clapping and cheering about your ministry, but God looks at the heart:

> I have found David the son of Jesse, a man after My
> own heart, who will do all My will. (Acts 13:22)

Is your ministry flourishing? Are people being saved, healed, and set free from bondage? Remember to be very careful not become prideful while operating in the gifts that God has blessed you with. When you see these accomplishments, rejoice in the Lord. However, it is important to remain humble and give all the glory to God because he is a jealous God and will not share his glory with anyone.

King Nebuchadnezzar became prideful when he saw that his kingdom, Babylon, had become a great nation. The king took all the glory for himself instead of praising God for his great accomplishment. When we are living in disobedience, God, in his mercies, always warns us and gives us time to repent before chastening us. He did the same thing with King Nebuchadnezzar. God gave the king a dream to warn him about his prideful heart, and God also showed him what would happen if he did not humble himself before the Lord. As the king was admiring his royal palace, he said to himself, "Is not this the great Babylon I have built as the royal residence, by my mighty power and for the glory of my majesty?"

> As the words were on his lips a voice came from heaven: "Your royal authority has been taken from you. You will be driven away from people and will live with the wild animals; you will eat grass like the ox. Seven times will pass by for you until you acknowledge that the Most High is sovereign over all kingdoms on earth and gives them to anyone he wishes." (Daniel 4:31–32)

God is the same God yesterday, today, and forevermore. Humble yourself before him. When ministering to God's people, it's uplifting to receive words of encouragement from others, but remember not to allow yourself to become prideful. You must watch your heart and not become puffed up. Do not think that being able to operate in different gifts makes you more spiritual than others.

As human beings, we have to make a habit of continuously commanding our hearts, our minds, and everything else that is within us to praise God and make sure to leave no room for the devil to come in. God focuses on our hearts and sees the motives behind everything we do. The gifts of God are in you. Do not to compete with other Christians. Do not boast about how much you're doing in comparison to others. We have all been blessed with different strengths, gifts, and talents. Let God be the judge. He is the Creator, and he only knows what everybody is made of.

Do not exalt yourself above others—lest you fall. Let's take the human body as an example. The feet may be able to run twenty miles, but without the eyes that are staying still watching and guiding where the feet are going, the race would not be a success:

> So then neither he who plants is anything, nor he who
> waters, but God who gives the increase. Now he who
> plants and he who waters are one, and each one will

receive his own reward according to his own labor. (1 Corinthians 3:7–8)

Everyone's gifts are valuable in God's eyes. Work in God's field as apostles, teachers, preachers, prophets, and evangelists, but always remain humble. We're all God's children. We all have the same goal of bringing those who are lost to God. In the end, we'll receive our rewards from God.

There are many people in the body of Christ who are hiding their gifts. Did you know that hiding your gift is not pleasing to God? Well, suppose you get up every Sunday morning and you go to church. Year after year, that's all you do. Did you know the devil attends church too? Going to church alone does not make you a Christian. It makes you a church attendee. Anyone can make it a routine to attend church, listen to the beautiful worship songs, clap once in a while when the music sounds great, listen to the sermon, and discuss it with friends. Many people go to church religiously and consume the church program as if it were a regular entertainment show that was put into place to please them and not God. However, their gifts and talents are never shared with the body of Christ.

As a new convert, it is a great start to make an effort to always be in a godly atmosphere where others are praising, worshipping, and serving God. However, if you truly belong to God, your heart will also be sensitive to the things that concern God. You will begin to feel the need to share your gifts and talents to glorify God. If that is not the case, make it a prayer point to ask God to give you a heart like his and be mindful of the things that are important to him.

When your heart is right before God, you become a blessing to others. God receives worship and pours out his blessings on you so you can always be a blessing to others. If you lack resources, struggle to meet deadlines, and live in poverty, you are under some sort of spiritual attack from the devil. He is the only one who wants to keep you down so the name of God won't be glorified through you.

Do you think God—who created the universe and owns everything that dwells in it—would want to see you suffer? God wants you to be blessed, be fruitful, have plenty, and take dominion over the earth because it is God's nature to see you prosper and possess everything good that will bring you joy. That is why he created all types of animals, plants, food, the moon, the sun, the sky, the planets, the oceans, the lands, and humankind with all different skin colors and features—black, white, and yellow.

> Then God saw everything that He had made, and indeed *it was* very good. So the evening and the morning were the sixth day. (Genesis 1:31)

However, because Satan is jealous, he does not want to see you enjoy life. He tries to corrupt everything that God has created. He created racism to make us hate each other and poisons the food we eat to bring sickness. Although the devil's schemes can be destructive, God has all power. He will protect us if we live in obedience to his will. Does your heart belong to Christ? He alone can protect and satisfy you:

> For I know the thoughts that I think toward you, says the Lord, thoughts of peace and not of evil, to give you a future and a hope. (Jeremiah 29:11)

CHAPTER 13

Lifestyle Accountability

If you are a born-again Christian—washed by the blood of Jesus Christ and saved by his grace—your conduct should be in alignment with who you say you are. True royals never have to waste time telling people that they are royalty. They don't need an introduction because their presence alone makes a huge difference when they walk into a room. They walk differently, they speak carefully, and they dress conservatively. Their mannerisms are so proper that you can quickly differentiate them from the other people in the crowd. Royals always want to act right because they do not want to do anything that will bring shame or dishonor to their kingdoms.

If the people who belong to earthly kingdoms know how to behave properly, how much more do those of us who belong to God's heavenly kingdom need to get our conduct right? If you have to go out of your way to tell people that you are a Christian, you have not been representing God in a godly manner. Christianity is a lifestyle.

Light remains light. Even if you put it in the middle of the darkness, everyone will see it. Light is not noisy, but it's so bright that it makes its presence known wherever it shows up. The Bible says we are the light, and if no one can see your light, that means you are in darkness—just like the rest of the people around you.

As a person who belongs to God, you have to be mindful of your behaviors because others are watching you, testing you, and judging you. You also have to be mindful of your motives because God knows everything. He sees your heart and the thoughts behind every action. Being accountable for your lifestyle helps you be good to yourself and to others. You cannot love others if you don't love God first and then love yourself.

Take care of yourself spiritually, mentally, emotionally, and physically—in that order.

"And you shall love the Lord your God with all your heart, with all your soul, with all your mind, and with all your strength." This is the first commandment. And the second, like it, is this: "You shall love your neighbor as yourself." There is no other commandment greater than these. (Mark 12:30–31)

Because we live in an imperfect body, it is almost impossible to do what is right at all time. Even Paul talked about his struggle in the Bible. At times, it can be difficult to do what's right.

> For what I am doing, I do not understand. For what I will to do, that I do not practice; but what I hate, that I do. (Romans 7:15)

Our sinful human nature does not make it easy to keep a perfect lifestyle, and being tempted by the devil regularly makes it even more challenging. Thank God the Holy Spirit is always here to help us, guide us, and strengthen us from any emotional, physical, spiritual, or mental attacks that come against us.

Life is like a battlefield, and God knew things were not going to be easy for humankind after the fall of Adam. God gave us principles to follow in order to be overcomers. How do we watch our behaviors and take accountability for our lifestyles so that we can remain strong and steady at all times?

> Put on the whole armor of God, that you may be able to stand against the wiles of the devil. For we do not wrestle against flesh and blood, but against principalities, against powers, against the rulers of the darkness of this age, against spiritual hosts of

wickedness in the heavenly places. Therefore take up the whole armor of God, that you may be able to withstand in the evil day, and having done all, to stand. Stand therefore, having girded your waist with truth, having put on the breastplate of righteousness, and having shod your feet with the preparation of the gospel of peace; above all, taking the shield of faith with which you will be able to quench all the fiery darts of the wicked one. And take the helmet of salvation, and the sword of the Spirit, which is the Word of God; praying always with all prayer and supplication in the Spirit, being watchful to this end with all perseverance and supplication for all the saint. (Ephesians 6:11–18)

You have to take accountability for your lifestyle because the Bible says you are the one who is going to stand before the throne of God to give an account of the life you have lived. No one is going to do it for you. There will be no judges or attorneys in heaven to speak on your behalf.

When we die, we can't take anything with us. If we could, the wealthiest and the richest of this world would make sure to win heaven all for themselves—and the poor would not even get a chance.

On Judgment Day, Jesus will be the only judge. Therefore, making excuses for yourself or blaming others for your downfall will not be accepted. Nothing can be hidden from Jesus because he is omniscient.

> So then each of us shall give account of himself to
> God. Therefore let us not judge one another anymore,
> but rather resolve this, not to put a stumbling block or
> a cause to fall in our brother's way. (Romans 14:12–13)

Take care of yourself spiritually, mentally, emotionally, and physically—in that order. How good can you be physically if you are lost spiritually, living far away from God, and being tormented by evil spirits? If you are oppressed by fear, depression, and anxiety, you will be mentally unstable and emotionally drained. Taking care of yourself spiritually is as important as waking up every day and making sure you have food to eat, a roof over your head, and clothes on your back.

God has all power and control over everything. The creations around you are proof that God exists. If you wake up one day and see a bunch of machines flying all over the country—and no one knows where they come from, but scientists claim that these machines are eliminating air pollution—would you bow down and worship the machines? Would you do some research to figure out who or what was behind the invention? When people worship the creations instead of God the Creator, it looks absurd to God. Creations worshiping creations is the devil's intention for you not to glorify God for who he is and what he has done:

> You shall not make for yourself a carved image—any likeness of anything that is in heaven above, or that is in the earth beneath, or that is in the water under the earth; you shall not bow down to them nor serve them. For I, the Lord your God, am a jealous God, visiting the iniquity of the fathers upon the children to the third and fourth generations of those who hate Me, but showing mercy to thousands, to those who love Me and keep My commandments. (Exodus 20:4–6)

Some people are enjoying the blessing of God and living in abundance because previous generations worshipped the true living God. The favor of the Creator is upon you. Other people are struggling in everything they do because previous generations lived in disobedience of God by worshiping idols.

You could be under a curse and not even know it. What should come to you easily turns into a battlefield. You could be struggling with your finances or health. You could be unable to finish what you start. You could have problems finishing school, getting married, or having children. You could always be getting in trouble with others. You could have so much debt you can't repay. You could be constantly battling fear, rejection, and disappointment. These obstacles are consequences for those who worship idols—and even their children will be affected. Many people blame God when they have to face these things because it looks so unfair that they have to deal with things they don't deserve. Do you ever wonder why there are people in jails for things they did not do? They could have associated with the wrong crowd, but most of the time, it is because a generational curse is following them.

What should you do to get your spiritual life in order? It may not be as easy as one, two, three. Some people are mad at God already. They are bitter about what they have been through or what they are going through. They don't want to hear about God because they're saying, "Where was God when all these bad things were happening? Why didn't he make them stop?"

God keeps his word. He cannot lie. He said idol worshipers would be cursed—and the iniquity of the fathers upon the children would endure into the third and fourth *generations* of those who hate him. That statement will be true forever. God is also merciful, and that is why he gives us grace. The devil's plan is for you to stay blinded and not see what's really going on. He wants you to live in bondage to sin and not break the generational curse. God sent his only begotten Son, Jesus Christ, to die on the cross for the remission of sins so that we all can be set free from the burden of sin:

Come to Me, all you who labor and are heavy laden,
and I will give you rest. Take My yoke upon you and
learn from Me, for I am gentle and lowly in heart, and
you will find rest for your souls. For My yoke is easy
and My burden is light. (Matthew 11:28–30)

Once your spiritual life is in good shape, everything else will follow. God's grace is for everyone who believes in him. It's for the rich and the poor and the weak and the strong. Are you living under God's grace today? Do you know what it really means to live under the grace of God? A baby prince who was lost at birth and adopted by a poor family in a different country would grow up to live in poverty and not know he was royalty. He would beg for food, wear dirty clothes, labor for low wages, and be mistreated, neglected, and abused. For this lost prince, misery is his norm and his reality.

On a glorious day, the king was visiting the country. He was passing though the poorest city, and he saw a young man digging in trash cans for leftover drinks and food. He had not showered for years. From far away, the king recognized the young man as his lost son because he looks exactly like him, and they both have the same birthmark on their faces. The king released a loud cry and called the young man by a name he had never heard before. The young man did not even turn around because he had lost his true identity. He did not answer to that name, and he thought there was no way on earth the king would be interested in him. The young man kept digging in the trash cans.

The king ran toward the young man with wide-open arms to hug him.

When the lost prince saw the king coming, he started to run away and hide because he thought he was in trouble.

The king yelled, "I am your father. I love you. Stop running away from me. I have plans for you to prosper. You were lost, but now I have found you. Come back to me. I will give you much more than you can ever think or imagine."

Sin brings you far away from God's grace and favor. In sin, you lose your true identity, privileges, and honor. You don't know that you are royalty, therefore you accept to live in poverty and darkness far away from God. In sin, the devil will mistreat you, neglect you, use you, abuse you, and torment you.

> My sheep hear My voice, and I know them, and they
> follow Me. And I give them eternal life, and they shall
> never perish; neither shall anyone snatch them out of
> My hand. (John 10:27–28)

The lost prince heard the king's voice and somehow recognized the voice. He stopped running, turned around, and started walking slowly toward the king. The lost prince was still in disbelief.

The king stretched out his hands and said, "Come to me, my son."

They hugged and cried. Everyone who knew the life the young man was living was shocked. They all wished they had treated him differently. The king took the prince to the palace, cleansed him, clothed him in royal garments, and fed him. Although the prince was cleansed and wearing royal garments, he was still afraid to touch things, ask for things, or give orders to those who were assigned to his service.

Do you know what it really means to live under the grace of God? If you have been born again and washed by the blood of Jesus Christ, you need to fully live in his abundant grace. When you are under his grace, angels are assigned to you. They are working on your behalf day and night. You have authority over the devil. Your life should reflect God's glory. You should not live in darkness or poverty or experience any type of bondage. You should be set free from any of the enemy's attacks. You should walk in victory and not in defeat. You should be the head and not the tail. That's the true living Word of God in your life.

God's Grace

In Him we have redemption through His blood, the forgiveness of sins, according to the riches of His grace. (Ephesians 1:7)

Let us therefore come boldly to the throne of grace, that we may obtain mercy and find grace to help in time of need. (Hebrews 4:16)

But He gives more grace. Therefore He says: "God resists the proud, But gives grace to the humble." (James 4:6)

But as you abound in everything—in faith, in speech, in knowledge, in all diligence, and in your love for us—see that you abound in this grace also. (2 Corinthians 8:7)

And the Word became flesh and dwelt among us, and we beheld His glory, the glory as of the only begotten of the Father, full of grace and truth. (John 1:14)

Therefore, having been justified by faith, we have peace with God through our Lord Jesus Christ. (Romans 5:1)

For by grace you have been saved through faith, and that not of yourselves; it is the gift of God, 9 not of works, lest anyone should boast. (Ephesians 2:8–9)

CHAPTER 14

Kingdom Production

One of the hardest battles in life is the fight for your true identity. Once you realize or discover who God says you are, what he created you for, your unique purpose, your gifts, your talents, your full potential, your strength, your capabilities, your divine assignment, and the knowledge of everything that is written by God for you to fulfill here on earth, you are a huge threat to the kingdom of darkness. The devil will try to kill you as fast as he can, but God always protects his children. Before Jesus was born, the prophet of God wrote about his birth:

> Therefore the Lord Himself will give you a sign Listen carefully the virgin will conceive and give birth to a son and she will call His name Emmanuel God is with us. (Isaiah 7:14)

In Matthew 1, we see that His name shall be called Jesus. He will save people from their sins, and Immanuel, which means God, is with us. You can understand why King Herod felt threatened by baby Jesus and tried to kill him because baby Jesus was born a Ruler and a Savior.

The devil secretly wants to destroy you because he knows there's greatness in you. You might not even know it, especially if you are a still a baby spiritually. God will always assign his angels to protect you. Pray that your eyes will be opened to see the greatness that God placed in you. If you are drained mentally, emotionally, and physically, it's time to rise, take your rightful place, and know who you are. To be productive in God's kingdom, you must know who you are. Otherwise, you're just wasting time, money, and energy, and at the end of your journey, you'd have nothing to show for it. Kingdom production starts once you start living for God on purpose. Do you know who God says you are?

Kingdom production begins after you have gone through the desert—where your faith and righteousness can be tested—and have passed the test.

What is man that You are mindful of him, And the son of man that You visit him? For You have made him a little lower than the angels, And You have crowned him with glory and honor. You have made

him to have dominion over the works of Your hands;

You have put all things under his feet. (Psalm 8:4–6)

God says you are a little lower than the angels. You are crowned with glory and honor, and God put everything under your feet. Meditate on these words. Do you ever ask God to reveal to you what is written of you in his book so that you may live your life according to God's divine purpose? David prayed to God:

Sacrifice and offering You did not desire; My ears You have opened. Burnt offering and sin offering You did not require. Then I said, "Behold, I come; In the scroll of the book *it is* written of me. I delight to do Your will, O my God, And Your law *is* within my heart." (Psalm 40:6–8)

When your heart's desire is to do God's will, you don't jump on the bandwagon and do what everyone else is doing. You can't be pressured to become someone you are not because God won't accept anything fake, artificial, manmade, copycatted, or unoriginal. God emphasized this so much in all his creations. Everything he created is unique. Even identical twins are not the same. They may look alike, but they are not the same people. When you try to be something other than what God created you to be, it does not bring glory to him. Being who God says you are is the first step toward accomplishing kingdom productivity.

Ever since you were born, the devil has been trying to make you lose your identity by trying to mess up God's plan for your life. When Satan went and tempted Jesus in the desert, the first thing he did was question Jesus's identity:

> Now when the tempter came to Him, he said, "If You are the Son of God, command that these stones become bread." (Matthew 4:3)

Satan knew exactly who Jesus was, but he wanted to tempt Jesus to see if he could mess up God's plan. Whenever you are being tempted by the devil, keep in mind that he is not doing this just for fun. The devil is tempting you because he sees God's beautiful plan for your life. He is going to do whatever it takes to see if you will come into agreement with him and mess it up. Since you have free will, you can choose to obey God and live a life of abundance or choose to live in disobedience and give legal access to the devil to torment you whenever he wants to.

> But he answered and said, it is written, Man shall not live by bread alone, but by every word that proceeded out of the mouth of God (Matthew 4:4)

Jesus came down and lived as a man to be an example for all of us so therefore follow his examples and no one else. Jesus's ministry started right after he passed all his tests from being tempted by the devil. So many ministers are not yet ready because they have not gone through the process yet. There are so many scandals in church because these ministers are not ready. They are making disciples, preaching, and getting fame right before their time, and the devil knows it. Satan is just waiting and planning how he's going to come after these premature ministers because he knows they are still weak in the flesh.

Let's follow Jesus's examples and save the body of Christ some hardship. The Son of God went through the process. You are called and chosen—but wait for God's timing to put you on display. Don't start thinking about getting deeply involved in ministry and kingdom production if you have not yet gone through the desert where your faith and righteousness can be tested.

Jesus's Time Line Concerning Ministries

In Matthew 4:1–11, Satan tempted Jesus. After he passed the temptation test, Jesus began to preach (Matthew 4:17, Matthew 4:18–21). He called his disciples, and his healing ministry started (Matthew 4:23–25). His kingdom production went viral:

Then His fame went throughout all Syria; and they brought to Him all sick people who were afflicted with various diseases and torments, and those who were demon-possessed, epileptics, and paralytics; and He healed them. Great multitudes followed Him from Galilee, and *from* Decapolis, Jerusalem, Judea, and beyond the Jordan. (Matthew 4:24–25)

You don't need to promote yourself when you start ministering to people for God's kingdom. All you need is God's power and anointing. Jesus called his disciples, but the crowd followed him because his presence carried healing, deliverance, miracles, signs, and wonders. The people who were delivered and those who witnessed the miracles were all in awe. They could not contain the joy and excitement about seeing a man who could turn water into wine, who had power over demons, who healed all diseases, who spoke to the raging sea, who calmed the storm, who fed five thousand men with five loaves of bread and two fish, and who had power over death and raised Lazarus from the dead four days after his burial! No human being would ever be able to keep their mouth shut after witnessing all those mind-blowing miracles. That's how Jesus did it. He never promoted himself. God the Father sent him. Before you start ministering to others, be sure that you've received the baptism of the Holy Spirit and fire. John the Baptist said,

> I indeed baptize you with water unto repentance, but
> He who is coming after me is mightier than I, whose
> sandals I am not worthy to carry. He will baptize you
> with the Holy Spirit and fire. (Matthew 3:11)

Once you start doing ministry, you enter a different realm. You enter the realm of the spirit. You cannot go into the realm of the spirit with your natural abilities or qualities. You must have legal passage or authorization; otherwise, you will be mocked and beaten by evil spirits. The realm of the spirit is not for lukewarm, passive, casual Christians.

You need to have the Holy Spirit and be on fire for God. Good preaching with superb articulation won't do it, and good singing with beautiful voices and music won't do it. You need to have the power of the Holy Ghost. When you open your mouth to preach and sing, your voice will shift the atmosphere, and demons will have to flee back to hell. When you lay hands on the sick, the spirit of infirmity will have to leave the person's body. It takes a relationship and intimacy with God.

The apostle Paul had a deep relationship with God. The anointing was so strong in him that his handkerchiefs or aprons were brought from his body to the sick—and they were healed. Those who were trying to imitate him were wounded by evil spirits:

Now God worked unusual miracles by the hands of Paul, that even handkerchiefs or aprons were brought from his body to the sick, and the diseases left them, and the evil spirits went out of them. Then some of the itinerant Jewish exorcists took it upon themselves to call the name of the Lord Jesus over those who had evil spirits, saying, "We exorcise you by the Jesus whom Paul preaches." Also, there were seven sons of Sceva, a Jewish chief priest, who did so. And the evil spirit answered and said, "Jesus I know, and Paul I know; but who are you?" Then the man in whom the evil spirit was leaped on them, overpowered them, and prevailed against them, so that they fled out of that house naked and wounded. This became known both to all Jews and Greeks dwelling in Ephesus; and fear fell on them all, and the name of the Lord Jesus was magnified. (Acts 19:11–17)

CHAPTER 15

Do You Have Power?

For I am not Ashamed of the Gospel of Christ, because
it is the power of God to salvation for everyone who
believes, for the Jew first and also the Greek.

—Romans 1:16

Do you have power? How do you get it? If the answer is no, you need

to go in prayer and ask God to bless you with his presence. Don't pray

for power. Instead, pray for his presence because his presence carries

the anointing—and you can only receive the anointing through the

Holy Spirit.

Without the presence of the Holy Spirit, you can only operate in

the flesh or be influenced by evil spirits. You must pray to let God

know that you need more of him. You must pray for the Holy Spirit to come and dwell in your life. Jesus instructed the disciples not to leave Jerusalem, but they had to wait to receive power first.

When God calls you into ministry, he is not going to send you out without giving you power first. God is omniscient, and he knows how dangerous it is to operate in the spiritual realm without his power. You don't have to be afraid and run away from your calling. Many people run away from their callings because they are focusing on their natural abilities. You are not going to make it; you must learn how to wait for God's timing.

Many people get excited when they receive insights from God for their lives. They run away and start doing ministry on their own because they're impatient and don't want to wait on God. Jerusalem was the disciples' hometown, and Jesus advised them to not go there before their time. The waiting period is very important, and it will determine how fast your ministry will grow, how far you will go, and how long your ministry will last. How many times do you see a ministry growing so rapidly and then dying as quickly as it came out? Don't skip the waiting period because a ministry without the power of God will not last. How do you receive power?

> *The waiting period is very important, and it will determine how fast your ministry will grow, how far you will go, and how long your ministry will last.*

> But you will receive power when the Holy Spirit comes
> on you; and you will be my witnesses in Jerusalem,
> and in all Judea and Samaria, and to ends of the earth.
> (Acts 1:8)

> Not by might, not by power, but by my Spirit, Says the
> Lord Almighty. (Zacharia 4:6)

You should not go out on your own terms to do ministry. This is not going to get done by your own might or strength. The Holy Spirit will fill you up—and you will receive power. You and I have the Gospel today because the disciples were obedient and waited on God's promise to receive the Holy Spirit.

> And they were all filled with the Holy Spirit and
> began to speak with other tongues, as the Spirit gave
> them utterance. (Acts 2:4)

You will know you have received the power of the Holy Spirit because the evidence will be clear. You won't have to question it because God's supernatural power surpasses all things. Those who were incompetent become competent, those who were timid become bold, and those who were afraid become brave.

The power of the Holy Spirit transforms people, and the people who used to know you will be in awe because the labels they used to put on you no longer resemble you. The box they used to keep you in no longer fits the new you. You will burst out because the power of God is too strong in your life—and not even you can contain the magnitude of God's presence. You have no choice but get out and release some of that power to others. You will become contagious, and those who link up with you will receive it as well. However those who want to remain in darkness will start to walk away from your life.

God might ask you to relocate and give you brand-new surroundings because positive plus negative equals negative. God wants to bring more positivity to your life so you can remain positive. Whenever God is getting ready to greatly bless someone, he asks them to relocate. For example, let's take what the Lord said to Abraham:

> Now the Lord had said to Abram: "Get out of your country, From your family And from your father's house, To a land that I will show you. I will make you a great nation; I will bless you And make your name great; And you shall be a blessing. I will bless those who bless you, And I will curse him who curses you; And in you all the families of the earth shall be blessed." (Genesis 12:1–3)

CHAPTER 16

Reward Day in Heaven

Have you ever thought about how the kind of life you live here on earth is extremely meaningful and valuable to God's kingdom? Do you ever question why we invest so much money, time, and energy on our physical bodies, which will one day perish, and not so much on our souls, which are eternal?

How can we be motivated to invest more in eternity? The best way to do that is by constantly reminding ourselves that the body is simply a temporary cover that makes it possible for us to function on earth. If the body becomes sick and is not able to recover, it will, unfortunately, be departed—and it will return to dust where it belongs.

As for man, his days are like grass; As a flower of the field, so he flourishes. For the wind passes over it, and it is gone, and its place remembers it no more. (Psalm

103:15–16)

The ground has no reward for our mortal bodies. After death, the decaying body gets eaten by worms and insects. However, the soul is eternal. It will separate itself from the body after death—and it will be rejoicing in paradise with Jesus Christ. There will be no more pain, sorrow, or suffering. There will only be eternal joy—forever and ever.

> He will wipe away every tear from their eyes, and death
> shall be no more, neither shall there be mourning, nor
> crying, nor pain anymore, for the former things have
> passed away. (Revelation 21:4)

The Word of God also makes us aware that there will be eternal punishment and absolute anguish in hell for the unrepentant souls who don't accept Jesus Christ as Lord and Savior.

> But the cowardly, unbelieving, abominable, murderers,
> sexually immoral, sorcerers, idolaters, and all liars shall
> have their part in the lake which burns with fire and
> brimstone, which is the second death. (Revelation 21:8)

Many people want to debate the Holy Word or try to change its context by adding their opinions to something that is far greater than them to accommodate their sinful natures. Some are living in denial or choosing to believe that hell does not exist.

If good and evil exist, where does the good come from—and where does bad come from? They cannot come from the same place, and they cannot end up in the same destination..

You may ask why would a loving God send anyone to a place where there is eternal anguish? God is love, and hate is not welcome in his presence. God is truth, and liars are not welcome in his presence. God is pure and holy, and the wicked and unrighteous are not welcome in his presence. Hell was not meant for humankind, but after Adam and Eve disobeyed God and ate from the tree of the knowledge of good and evil, sin entered:

> And the Lord God said, Behold, the man is become as one of us, to know good and evil: and now, lest he put forth his hand, and take also of the tree of life, and eat, and live forever: Therefore the Lord God sent him forth from the garden of Eden, to till the ground from whence he was taken. (Genesis 3:22–23)

The Bible makes it clear that human beings get to choose how we live our lives on earth. We have the knowledge and understanding of good and evil. It is not a matter of God sending people to hell because he does not like them or bringing people to heaven because he favors them. There is no favoritism in God's kingdom.

The way we choose to live on earth will determine where our souls end up at the end of our journeys. We all have the freedom to choose how we want to live our lives here on earth, however we must choose wisely. God knows all about our sinful nature, God knows the devil tried to mess it up for us, but God has the final say! He loves us so much, and he does not want to see any of us perish in the eternal lake of fire.

> And I will put enmity between thee and the woman,
> and between thy seed and her seed; it shall bruise thy
> head, and thou shalt bruise his heel. (Genesis 3:15)

Glory be to God that he always keeps his word! He demonstrated it to us by sending his only Son, Jesus, to die for our sins. All we must do is repent from our sins and accept Jesus Christ into our hearts as our Lord and Savior:

> For God so loved the world, that he gave his only
> begotten Son, that whosoever believeth in him should
> not perish, but have everlasting life. (John 3:16)

What happens after your conversion, you receive the Holy Spirit, and after you start living for God? What will happen to all your good work, your good deeds, your faithfulness, and all the souls you bring to God along the way? Let us check out some Bible facts about being rewarded in heaven.

> Each one's work will become clear; for the Day will declare it, because it will be revealed by fire; and the fire will test each one's work, of what sort it is. (1 Corinthians 3:13–14)

> But lay up for yourselves treasures in heaven, where neither moth nor rust destroys and where thieves do not break in and steal. (Matthew 6:20)

> Rejoice and be exceedingly glad, for great is your reward in heaven, for so they persecuted the prophets who were before you. (Matthew 5:12)

> Blessed is the man who endures temptation; for when he has been approved, he will receive the crown of life which the Lord has promised to those who love Him. (James 1:12)

Before we start thinking about receiving a reward from God, we all need to strive to remain humble while doing the work of the Lord. We must not become prideful or be tempted to boast about our giving and our service to others. Your good deeds cannot save you or give you a free passage to heaven; otherwise, all the rich men on earth would buy large portions of God's kingdom for themselves, their families, and their friends—like they do here on earth—and all the poor people would not even get a chance to access heaven's gate. Glory be to God! Jesus came and died and rose again for us all—the rich and the poor! God's kingdom is for whoever believes in Jesus. They will not perish and will have everlasting life (John 3:16).

Your good deeds are only acceptable to God if they are done with a pure heart and with the right motives.

> Therefore, if you bring your gift to the altar, and there remember that your brother has something against you, leave your gift there before the altar, and go your way. First be reconciled to your brother, and then come and offer your gift. (Matthew 5:23–24)

Your gifts, deeds, and worship mean nothing to God if you cannot live in peace and harmony with your brothers, sisters, and all those around you. When you joyfully bring your gift to God with the right motives and a pure heart, you will live a blessed life here on earth for being obedient in your giving—and you will also receive your reward in heaven.

Your good deeds are not limited to money. If that were the case, the poor would not have any reward in heaven. When God created you, he made you unique. Your gifts and talents are unique too. When we serve God and help others through our gifts and talents, it is a pure act of worship. Therefore, everything you do here on earth will reflect in eternity. God will reward everyone according to what they have done at the end of the earth journey. It pays off to be a good steward of what God has blessed you with.

Let us check into some Bible facts concerning the result of our generosity:

> Give, and it will be given to you: good measure, pressed down, shaken together, and running over will be put into your bosom. For with the same measure that you use, it will be measured back to you. (Luke 6:38)

Bring ye all the tithes into the storehouse, that there may be meat in mine house, and prove me now herewith, saith the Lord of hosts, if I will not open you the windows of heaven, and pour you out a blessing, that there shall not be room enough to receive it. (Malachi 3:10)

> Motives and how to give way to give: Take heed that ye do not your alms before men, to be seen of them: otherwise ye have no reward of your Father which is in heaven. Therefore, when thou doest thine alms, do not sound a trumpet before thee, as the hypocrites do in the synagogues and in the streets, that they may have glory of men. Verily I say unto you, They have their reward. But when thou doest alms, let not thy left hand know what thy right hand doeth: That thine alms may be in secret: and thy Father which seeth in secret himself shall reward thee openly. (Matthew 6:1–4)

> When the Son of man shall come in his glory, and all the holy angels with him, then shall he sit upon the throne of his glory: And before him shall be gathered all nations: and he shall separate them one from another, as a shepherd divideth his sheep from the goats: And he shall set the sheep on his right hand,

but the goats on the left. Then shall the king say unto them on his right hand, Come, ye blessed of my Father, inherit the kingdom prepared for you from the foundation of the world: For I was an hungred, and ye gave me meat: I was thirsty, and ye gave me drink: I was a stranger, and ye took me in: Naked, and ye clothed me: I was sick, and ye visited me: I was in prison, and ye came unto me. Then shall the righteous answer him, saying, Lord, when saw we thee an hungred, and fed thee? or thirsty, and gave thee drink? When saw we thee a stranger, and took thee in? or naked, and clothed thee? Or when saw we thee sick, or in prison, and came unto thee? And the king shall answer and say unto them, Verily I say unto you, In as much as ye have done it unto one of the least of these my brethren, ye have done it unto me. Then shall he say also unto them on the left hand, Depart from me, ye cursed, into everlasting fire, prepared for the devil and his angels: For I was an hungred, and ye gave me no meat: I was thirsty, and ye gave me no drink: I was a stranger, and ye took me not in: naked, and ye clothed me not: sick, and in prison, and ye visited me not. Then shall they also answer him, saying, Lord, when saw we thee an hungred, or athirst, or a stranger, or naked, or sick, or in prison, and did not minister unto thee? Then shall he answer them, saying, Verily I say unto you, In as much as ye did it not to one of the least of these, ye did it not to me. And these shall go away into everlasting punishment: but the righteous into life eternal. (Matthew 25:31–46)

Does the soul go to paradise immediately after death? Let us look at a few Bible verses:

The Penitent Thief

And he said unto Jesus, Lord, remember me when thou comest into thy kingdom. And Jesus said unto him, Verily I say unto thee, today shalt thou be with me in paradise. (Luke 23:42–43)

Lazarus and the Rich Man

And in hell he lifts up his eyes, being in torments, and seeth Abraham afar off, and Lazarus in his bosom. And he cried and said, Father Abraham, have mercy on me, and send Lazarus, that he may dip the tip of his finger in water, and cool my tongue; for I am tormented in this flame. But Abraham said, Son, remember that thou in thy lifetime receivedst thy good things, and likewise Lazarus evil things: but now he is comforted, and thou art tormented. And beside all this, between us and you there is a great gulf fixed: so that they which would pass from hence to you cannot; neither can they pass to us, that would come from thence. (Luke 16:22–25)

Judgment Day

Verily, verily, I say unto you, He that heareth my word, and believeth on him that sent me, hath everlasting life, and shall not come into condemnation; but is passed from death unto life. (John 5:24)

Printed in the United States
By Bookmasters